Chinese
ART &
CULTURE

Clare Hibbert

Raintree

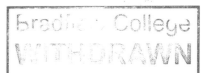

www.raintreepublishers.co.uk
Visit our website to find out more information about **Raintree** books.

To order:

 Phone 44 (0)1865 888113

 Send a fax to 44 (0)1865 314091

 Visit the Raintree bookshop at **www.raintreepublishers.co.uk** to browse
our catalogue and order online.

 Produced for Raintree by
White-Thomson Publishing Ltd
Bridgewater Business Centre, 210 High Street,
Lewes, East Sussex, BN7 2NH.

First published in Great Britain by Raintree, Halley Court, Jordan Hill, Oxford OX2 8EJ,
part of Harcourt Education.
Raintree is a registered trademark of Harcourt Education Ltd.

© Harcourt Education Ltd 2005
First published in paperback in 2006
The moral right of the proprietor has been asserted.

Editorial: Kay Barnham, Nicole Irving, and Louise Galpine
Design: Simon Borrough and Ron Kamen
Illustrations: Tinstar Design
Picture Research: Elaine Fuoco-Lang
Production: Amanda Meaden

Originated by Ambassador Litho Ltd
Printed and bound in China by South China Printing Company

ISBN 1 844 21055 3 (hardback)   ISBN 1 844 21060 X (paperback)
09 08 07 06 05   10 09 08 07 06
10 9 8 7 6 5 4 3 2 1   10 9 8 7 6 5 4 3 2 1

British Library Cataloguing in Publication Data
Hibbert, Clare
    World Art and Culture: Chinese
    709.5'1
A full catalogue record for this book is available from the British Library.

Acknowledgements
The publishers would like to thank the following for permission to reproduce photographs:
Art Archive pp. **6**, **21**, pp. **16**, **27** (Genius of China Exhibition), **29** (National Palace Museum, Taiwan/HarperCollins Publishers); Bridgeman Art
Library p. **14**; British Museum pp. **34**, **41**, **47** (The Trustees of the British Museum); Cleveland Museum p. **30**; Corbis pp. **33** (Alan Levenson), **22**
(Arthur Rothstein), **18**, **20** (Asian Art & Archaeology, Inc), **37** (Burstein Collection), **31** (Carl & Ann Purcell), **8**, **36**, **38** (Christie's Images), **42** (David
G Houser), **26** (David Cumming; Eye Ubiquitous), **43** (Dean Conger), **45** (Karen Su), **7** (Lawrence Manning), **49** (Massimo Listri), **39** (Massimo
Mastrorillo), **46** (Peter Beck), **1**, **17** (Royal Ontario Museum), **11** (Tiziana and Gianni Baldizzone); Harcourt/Corbis pp. **9**, **10**, **13**, **15**; Kobal Collection
Art Archive Travelsite Advertising Archive p.**51**; TopFoto.co.uk pp. **5**, **19** (The British Museum/HIP); Werner Forman Archive pp. **40** (British
Library, London), **50** (Christian Deydier, London), **23**, **25**, **28**, **32**, **35**; WTPix p. **12** (Chris Fairclough).

Cover photograph of mask reproduced with kind permission of Corbis/Freelance Consulting Services Pty Ltd. and of fabric, reproduced with kind
permission of Bridgeman Art Library

The publishers would like to thank Louise Tythacott for her assistance in the preparation of this book.

'q' is pronounced like 'ch' in 'china'
'x' is pronounced like 'sh' in 'sheep'
'zh' is pronounced like 'j' in 'jump'

Contents

Words printed in the text in bold, **like this**, are explained in the Glossary.

Introduction

China is the world's fourth-largest country, after Russia, Canada, and the USA. Part of eastern Asia, it covers an area of nearly 10 million square kilometres (4 million square miles). China is a country of contrasts, with towering mountain peaks and endless plains, bleak deserts and teeming tropical forests.

To the north and northwest, China is bordered by desert. To the west lies Tibet, with mountain ranges including the mighty Himalayas. The gentle slopes of southwestern China are covered with **bamboo** forests, home to the rare giant panda. Further south is Yunnan province's Stone Forest – craggy outcrops of weathered limestone that look like giant tree trunks.

Mighty rivers

Three great rivers cross China from west to east, watering fertile plains and valleys. They are the Huang He (Yellow River), the Yangzi (Changjiang or 'long river'), and the Xi Jiang. At 6300 kilometres (3900 miles), the Yangzi is China's longest river.

Chinese civilization formed along the banks of the second-longest river, the Huang He. This river is also known as the Yellow River because it sometimes silts up with loose, yellow soil called **loess**, which is blown from deserts to the west. Loess is an important ingredient in Chinese **ceramics**.

Modern China is divided into regions called provinces. The capital city is Beijing. Hong Kong was a former British colony, but became a Special Administrative Region of China in 1997.

4

This beautiful Ming **dynasty** bowl dates from the early 17th century. It was found in Jingdezhen, Jiangxi province, in southern China.

The people

Most of China's population is Han Chinese. Han people share the same written language but speak different **dialects**, such as Cantonese. Mandarin, today known as *putonghua* or the *common language*, is the standard form of spoken Chinese. A large number of **ethnic** minorities lives in China, including the Mongols, Tibetans, Dong and Uygurs. More than 50 minority languages are spoken.

China's population of 1.25 billion is concentrated in the east. Although many people live in big cities or towns, most remain in the countryside. Western China is very thinly populated.

Arts and crafts

China's civilization stretches back thousands of years. Some of its earliest art included pottery (5000 BCE), **jade** (4500 BCE), and bronze vessels (1500 BCE). The country is famous for its ceramics, especially **porcelain**. Long before many other countries began to use mass production techniques, Chinese craftworkers made items in this way. Each stage of an item's production was performed by a different person, allowing many items to be made quickly. China's physical geography kept it isolated from the rest of the world. With few outside influences, art and society developed in different ways from those of the rest of the world.

Art remains part of everyday life in China. This book explores different aspects of Chinese art, such as silk, ceramics, and calligraphy, and concentrates on individual works within these groupings. By looking at examples from different moments in China's history and from different geographical regions, it aims to build up a picture of the rich heritage of Chinese art.

Early China

The first farming villages were settled along the Huang He around 7000 BCE, by people who knew how to craft tools from stone, wood, and bone. Within 2000 years, these people were making pottery. They learned how to work copper around 2000 BCE and, soon after, their Bronze Age began.

Slowly, some families grew more powerful than others and began to rule over areas of land. Around 1500 BCE, the Shang dynasty came to power. They ruled over China for nearly 450 years. Around 1050 BCE, the Shang were defeated by the Zhou, who controlled China until 221 BCE. Towards the end of their rule, the land was split into lots of smaller states, which were often at war with each other.

China under the emperors

China was finally united in 221 BCE by the first Qin emperor, Qin Shi Huangdi. A strong ruler, he made changes to China that helped it to remain powerful and united, even after his death.

Over the centuries, many different dynasties rose and fell, but China remained an imperial country (ruled by an emperor) until the end of the Qing dynasty in 1911. However, during the 19th century, the seaport of Shanghai became a base for the British, French and Japanese.

During his reign as emperor of all China (221–207 BCE), Qin Shi Huangdi oversaw building projects that included roads, canals, and the Great Wall. He also established a common written language, to be used by all his people. This portrait was painted in the 18th century.

BCE	7000–1500, Neolithic Age: pottery making and carving. *c.*1500–1050, Shang dynasty: bronze-working begins. Earliest writing on **oracle bones**.	1050–221, Zhou dynasty: birth of **Confucianism** and **Daoism**. 221–207, Qin Shi Huangdi unites China and standardizes writing. **Terracotta** army.	206 BCE – 220 CE, Han dynasty: large-scale production of bronzes, **lacquerware**, ceramics, and textiles. Paper invented. Confucianism is state 'religion'.

Many Chinese homes contain a special sacred place or shrine. Here a bust of Mao Zedong sits among offerings to the family's ancestors.

After the emperors

Following the collapse of the Qing, China had a troubled time. There were invasions by the Japanese and two world wars. Above all, there was a long struggle for power between the two main political parties, the Communists and the Nationalists. Finally, the Communists won. Their leader, Mao Zedong, established the People's Republic of China on 1 October 1949.

Communist China

Under the Communists, Chinese society was completely reorganized. At first, the Communists banned customs and **rituals** that had belonged to imperial times. They wanted to foster new art forms, such as grand new buildings, heroic statues, eye-catching posters, and **patriotic** plays. For a time, any art form that did not express the ideals of the government was banned. Gradually, though, society in China has become more open again. Communist leaders now permit traditional arts, crafts, and music.

CE 618–906, Tang dynasty: golden age of poetry, painting, and sculpture. **Buddhism** flourishes. Woodblock printing invented.

960–1279, Song dynasty: pottery and painting thrive. Ancient bronzes and jades catalogued. Chinese opera and shadow puppet plays emerge.

1279–1368, Yuan dynasty: Mongol Yuan emperors encourage building, silks, ceramics and lacquerware. Chinese scholar-poets.

Beliefs

The Chinese do not have one single religion but follow several different sets of beliefs. The earliest Chinese worshipped many different gods and spirits, including the spirits of their own dead ancestors. Ceremonies involving ancestor worship are still practised today. As well as these popular beliefs, the Chinese also follow **Confucianism**, **Daoism**, and **Buddhism**.

Confucianism

The teachings of Confucius (551–479 BCE) were adopted by the Han dynasty in the 3rd century CE. Confucius was a **philosopher** who wrote about how an ordered society could be achieved. He stressed, for example, how a man should be obeyed by his wife and children. In the same way, he thought that people should obey their emperor.

Daoism

Lao Zi was another philosopher, who lived around the same time as Confucius. His teachings form the basis of Daoism. He believed in the dao – the 'way' – and said that people could follow the dao by living in harmony with nature. By doing this they might reach supreme understanding and achieve the state of immortality, or existing for ever.

In Daoist tradition there are Eight **Immortals**, whose lives inspire other Daoists. Ho Hsiang-ku, the only female immortal, lived like a hermit in the mountains. Many Daoists followed her example, choosing to live alone on remote mountains where they could spend their time quietly thinking about nature.

Daoism had a big influence on Chinese landscape painters. *Waiting to Cross a River in Autumn* by Zhang Lu (above) dates back to the 15th century.

1368–1644, Ming dynasty: fine porcelain, poetry, and painting. Building of Forbidden City and development of garden design.

1644–1911, Qing dynasty: many painting styles. Carved lacquerware, painted porcelain, and rich silk embroidery.

1911: Republicans oust the emperor. Civil war follows.

The orderliness of Confucianism influenced all aspects of Chinese culture, including traditional architecture, where building complexes were laid out according to strict rules.

Buddhism

Siddhartha Gautama (485–405 BCE) was an Indian prince who later became known as the Buddha, or the Enlightened One. He founded the religion of Buddhism, which reached China around 60 CE.

Buddhists believe that they can achieve nirvana (a state of supreme happiness) through **meditation** and by following the Eightfold Path. This is a set of eight rules that help people to live better lives. The Chinese developed their own branch of Buddhism, called Chan Buddhism, which stressed the importance of meditation.

Buddhism was at its most popular in China during the Tang dynasty (7th–10th century). A lot of beautiful religious art dates from this time, such as paintings or tapestries depicting the gods and demons that Buddhists believed in.

Religious art today

Although all religion was banned for a time in Communist China, religious beliefs are very much alive today. Artists paint gods on to banners or create posters of religious sayings in beautiful calligraphy. These are put up to mark special festivals, such as New Year. Modern-day ceramic and stone ornaments of Confucius, Lao Zi, and the Buddha are popular in people's homes, too.

Statues of the Buddha, like this one in Hong Kong, are found all over China.

1949: Communist leader Mao Zedong founds the People's Republic of China

1966–1976: Cultural Revolution spreads the Communist message and sees the arrest of many intellectuals

2001: China accepted into World Trade Organization

Architecture

In China, wood has always been the usual building material. Unfortunately, it does not last very well, so few ancient buildings survive. Bricks were used for some buildings, such as underground tombs.

China's Great Wall

The Great Wall of China is one of the most impressive building projects ever created. Stretching 6700 kilometres (4200 miles) across the north of the country, it was built to keep out marauding enemy tribes from the steppes (Central Asian grasslands). It started out as a collection of short walls, made of wood and piled-up earth. In the 210s BCE, the first Qin emperor, Qin Shi Huangdi, joined together the existing defences to form the Great Wall. It has a road running along the top, as well as regular lookout towers from which smoke-signal messages could be sent. Over the centuries, the Great Wall was rebuilt with strong stone – in some places it was covered with bricks. Today, it is a major tourist attraction.

Tomb architecture

From the 2nd century BCE, tombs were built from clay bricks that were fired in an oven to make them strong and waterproof. The tombs were enormous underground complexes of rooms and corridors, probably based on the layouts of above-ground palaces for the living. However, despite the vast scale, **artisans** paid attention to the smallest details. For example, many of the bricks they used were fired with decorative designs. Some bricks showed everyday scenes, while others featured a few figures, such as musicians, lovers, acrobats, or gods.

Cut into rock

On the Loess **Plateau**, the **loess** built up over thousands of years to create a soft sandstone that was easy to work. Here, from around 5000 BCE, people hollowed out cave-like homes. From the 4th century CE, **Buddhist** monasteries and temples were cut into the cliff faces in northern China.

Dong buildings

The Dong people of southern China still live in traditional two-storey wooden houses. The lower floor is used to house animals and store firewood, while the family lives on the upper floor.

Each Dong village also has a spectacular drum tower, like the one on the right, up to thirteen storeys high. From a distance, and because of its many overlapping roofs, the tower looks like a fir tree, which is sacred to the Dong people. The villagers paint the **eaves** of the drum tower to show myths, legends, and scenes of everyday life.

Traditional wooden homes and palaces

The traditional design for Chinese homes and palaces was a walled compound, which was carefully positioned so that each wall faced in one direction of the compass – the entrance was usually on the south wall. Within the compound, several generations of the same family might live in separate buildings.

Such designs date back at least as far as 25 CE. They continued to be built until 1911, the time of the last Chinese emperor.

 Eighteen-year trees

To celebrate the birth of a new child, Dong parents plant a grove of pine trees. They call these 'eighteen-year trees' because the trees will be ready to fell eighteen years later, just as the child becomes an adult. The trees will supply enough pine timber to build a home for them.

Following tradition

The most striking feature of traditional Chinese buildings is the overhanging roof. Most temples and palaces have a heavy, curved roof with broad eaves or double eaves. Architects support the roof's overhang with clever wooden brackets that spread the weight.

In 1103, a Song **dynasty** civil servant called Li Jie wrote a manual of architecture, recording techniques, measurements, and rules. At the time, there were eight different **ranks** of building – no house or public building could be built that was too grand for its owner or function.

Chinese buildings were usually painted. The walls were often red – a colour associated with life, wealth, energy, and summer – while the base was white, symbolizing death, autumn, and age.

The brackets were painted blue and green. Roof tiles were painted only on public or grand buildings and were usually yellow and green.

Today, most city-dwelling Chinese live in high-rise flats. However, some modern concrete houses have old-style overhanging roofs and, in many towns, newspaper kiosks are built to look like traditional **pavilions**.

This is one of the hundreds of buildings, including palaces and temples, in the Forbidden City in Beijing, which was home to the emperors of China for nearly 500 years and is now a museum. It is so called because no ordinary person or foreigner was allowed in without permission.

This Chinese courtyard garden is a small-scale version of a much larger landscape.

Pagodas

Pagodas are multi-storeyed towers built in Buddhist temple complexes that take the idea of overhanging roofs further. The Wooden Pagoda at Yingxian, in Shanxi province, was built during the 11th century CE and is one of the oldest wooden buildings in the world. It stands nine storeys high, and is held together entirely by wooden joints – there is not a single nail or screw!

In Xi'an, Shaanxi province, there are two famous pagodas. The Big Wild Goose Pagoda was originally built around 589 CE, but has been rebuilt many times since. The existing wood-and-brick structure, built during the Qing dynasty, stands 64 metres (210 feet) high. Not far away is the fifteen-tiered Little Goose Pagoda, finished in 709 CE. Both pagodas were built to house Buddhist scriptures brought from India. In recent years, architects have rebuilt ancient-style pagodas in an effort to keep old traditions alive.

Chinese gardens

The Chinese have two styles of garden – huge parks and small courtyards. Parkland is carefully cultivated to look wild and rugged. Pavilions, lakes, waterfalls, islands, bridges, trees, and boulders are all part of the design, which aims to create a natural-looking landscape.

Parks are planned as a series of beauty spots. Paths twist and turn to give surprise vistas, while benches and pavilions are sited to take advantage of a particular feature, such as the sound of water or the colours of the trees.

Tiny courtyard gardens are planned on the same principles, with pools and rocks representing natural lakes and mountains. Courtyard gardens are often designed to be seen through latticed windows. These frame the views into the garden, like a set of pictures.

Pottery and ceramics

The Chinese started to use a wheel to make pottery from clay around 4000 years ago. In the 7th or 8th century, they discovered a fine white clay that could be used to make **porcelain**. Elsewhere in the world porcelain is often known as 'china', because this is where it first came from.

Stone Age pottery

Even before they invented the potter's wheel, Chinese **artisans** were skilled potters. They coiled 'snakes' of clay into dishes or simply shaped the clay by hand. People who lived at Banpo, near Xi'an, between 4000 and 3000 BCE, are known as the 'painted pottery' people, because of their decorated earthenware pots.

Pottery styles varied from place to place. The 'black pottery' people lived near Shandong between 3500 and 2000 BCE. They made at least two different styles of pots. Their everyday pots were plain grey, while their best ones were made

Model ceramic farms like this one have been found in Chinese tombs from around the 2nd century BCE. The tomb's owner would have been a prosperous landowner.

of thin clay that was burnished black or red. These pots were so fragile that they were probably used only for special ceremonies or as ornaments.

Tomb pottery

During Qin and Han times, important people were often buried with pottery copies of the belongings they had used when they were alive. They thought that they might need these things in the next life. Many tombs contain clay models of buildings, such as farms and granaries, as well as rice fields, fishponds, and wells. There are also miniature farm animals, farm workers, servants, and entertainers.

Ordinary objects were also buried with the dead, such as **ceramic** dishes, storage jars, and lamps, often beautifully painted with symbolic animals or scenes. Tigers, dragons, and birds were used to depict the worlds of the **immortals**.

 Modern terracotta

Using a type of clay called **loess**, potters still work in **terracotta**. Some produce figures for tourists visiting Qin Shi Huangdi's terracotta warriors. The figures are beautifully crafted replicas of the original soldiers, only smaller, usually standing around 30 centimetres (12 inches) high.

Terracotta warriors

The tomb of the Qin emperor, Qin Shi Huangdi, is guarded by more than 7000 life-size clay soldiers, discovered in 1974. They were buried in pits, along with clay horses, weapons, and chariots made of bronze. Each soldier was put together from separately moulded body parts and then hand-finished. No two figures are exactly the same, they have different facial expressions or slightly different uniforms, and they are carefully arranged according to **rank**. Although the paint has faded, they would have been brightly coloured when they were first made, 2200 years ago.

Centres of ceramics

In ancient China, mined clay was taken to specialist pottery-making centres, where there were huge **kilns** used for **firing** ceramics. The wood-fired 'dragon' kiln was popular in the south of the country. It was narrow, extremely long, and could fire items at high temperatures (up to 1300 °C or 2370 °F). In the north, potters used the 'bread-roll' kiln. Small, round, high-roofed, and fuelled by coal, it too could reach high temperatures (up to 1370 °C or 2500 °F).

Finally, the 'egg-shaped' kiln was used in Jingdezhen, Jiangxi province. It was wood-fuelled and looked like half an egg, with a tall chimney attached. As it reached temperatures between 1000 °C and 1300 °C (1830 °F and 2370 °F), it was very **versatile**, and could be used to create many **glaze** effects.

Using glazes

Many of the finest Chinese ceramics are glazed. The potter applies a layer of powder to the clay. When fired, the powder melts to form a glassy, shiny glaze. Some glazes are clear, but most are coloured. Used from Han times, lead produced green and brown colours. Sometimes, spots of colour were applied beneath the glaze. Then the artist would apply the main glaze before firing.

Unglazed ceramics

However, not all of the best ceramics were glazed. Zisha wares from Yixing, in Jiangsu province, were admired for their simplicity. They were plain teapots and cups in unglazed brown **stoneware**, simply shaped by hand. Yixing is still famous for its teapots but also produces over 2000 different types of pottery, including replacement roof tiles for buildings in the Forbidden City, Beijing.

This glazed stoneware vase is decorated with buildings and **Daoist** immortals. It dates back to 265–316 CE and comes from Zhejiang province.

◇ Chinese clays

Three different types of clay are found in China. **Loess** is a browny-yellow clay from northern China, used for terracotta figures. Also from northern China are the sedimentary clays, such as **kaolin** and fire clay. Most Yixing pottery is made of kaolin. The very finest type of clay is white porcelain stone, which comes from southern China.

Figures and statues

Skilled Chinese potters can make ceramic statues that rival the most beautiful bronzes. Many old **Buddhist** temples include large painted figures. Despite their size, these were fired as single pieces in enormous kilns. Religious figures include statues of the Buddha and also his disciples, known as *luohans* or *arhats*.

Ornaments on show

Some figures are made purely for display in the home. Long ago, only the very wealthiest Chinese could afford such ceramics, but today they are popular across society. Small statues of ordinary people or activities are a speciality – for example, pairs of old men playing chess, fishermen holding fishing rods made of wood and string, dancers, and musicians. Some of these are made in simple, fired clay, while others are painted or glazed.

This glazed ceramic sculpture was made for a Buddhist temple in the 11th century. It shows an *arhat*, a disciple of the Buddha who has achieved nirvana.

◈ Coloured enamels

Enamels are made by mixing glass paste with metallic compounds that provide colour. Manganese oxide, for example, produces purple enamel. Enamels are used to decorate metalwork as well as ceramics. A bronze or copper pot is prepared by adding little sections of enamel paste, held in place by strips of metal. Then the whole pot is fired and the pastes melt to create a glassy finish. This technique is known as **cloisonné**.

This Ming **dynasty** porcelain jar dates back to the 1500s and is decorated with brightly coloured enamels. Less expensive jars were used for storage, while this jar was probably an ornament.

Made in 1610, this porcelain figure from Fujian province represents a Buddhist god.

Decorating porcelain

Porcelain was first developed during the Tang dynasty (7th–10th century). It was white, thin, and almost see-through. By the time of the Yuan dynasty (13th–14th century), the first blue-and-white porcelain was being produced.

Jingdezhen, in Jiangxi province, is still a major centre of ceramics but its most spectacular output was during Ming times (1368–1644). From the 14th century, it produced pure white porcelain decorated with hand-painted birds and flowers in blue. In the 16th century, artists painted on underglazes to create scenes of human figures in green, red, and blue.

Using enamels

From the 1600s, artisans often used **enamels** to colour their pieces. This style of decoration reached its height of popularity during the Qing dynasty and was known in the West as *famille rose, jaune, noire,* or *verte* (pink-, yellow-, black-, or green-family), depending on the main colour of the decoration. Using enamels, workshops turned out porcelain in vibrant colours that was also decorated in more detail. As well as painting birds, flowers, fruits, or fish, artisans created delicate scenes, such as ladies relaxing in gardens or scholars admiring a landscape.

Plain and simple

Although it took great skill to produce porcelain with **intricate** decorations, plainer pieces were also admired. The Song emperors favoured Ru ware, which had a crackled blue-green glaze. The third Ming emperor, Zhudi, was a great collector of plain white porcelain.

Today, many ceramics factories reproduce the most popular styles of the past. Everyday tableware is still commonly blue and white. Sometimes, tiny grains of rice have been pressed into the clay – these result in see-through spots and are used to create patterns or borders.

Metalworking

In China, the Bronze Age took place during the Shang **dynasty** (1500–1050 BCE). Bronze weapons were far sharper and easier to handle than earlier axeheads and spearheads made of stone. According to Chinese tradition, however, bronze **casting** began long before the Shang. Around 5000 years ago, the legendary emperor Yu is said to have split his empire into nine provinces and then cast a bronze tripod (three-legged pot) for each of them.

Three-legged bronze pots have been found by **archaeologists** that date back as far as 1400 BCE. They are parts of whole sets of different-shaped **ritual vessels**, which contained offerings to the spirits of dead ancestors. Each shape of pot was probably used for a particular food or wine. They were made for family temples and also buried in tombs.

Sichuan sculptures

Although the Shang, and later the Zhou, were skilful workers of bronze, they did not produce many bronze sculptures, and certainly none showing human figures. However, people living in southern China at that time did produce bronze figures.

In 1986, archaeologists discovered two pits full of offerings to the gods at Sanxingdui in Sichuan province. The pits contained burnt animal remains as well as bronze statues of human figures and more than 50 heads and masks. This bronze head was among them. No one is sure of the exact significance of the figures, but they were probably used in religious rituals of some sort.

Shang pots

In Shang times, ritual bronze vessels were usually decorated with **abstract** designs of lines, circles, and swirls. One popular style of decoration was the **taotie** motif – a stylized pattern that featured bulging 'eyes' like a monster's. The taotie monsters may have been made to watch out for evil spirits, but their exact meaning is a mystery today.

This Shang bronze wine vessel has a taotie pattern of abstract eyes.

Zhou pots

During the Zhou dynasty (1050–221 BCE) people continued to use sets of bronze vessels. Zhou pots are often cast in the same shapes as those made during the Shang dynasty, but their decoration is completely different. Instead of abstract designs, there are intricate birds, coiled dragons, or elephants. The Zhou also inscribed the inside of their pots, giving information about the owner of the pot, his achievements, and the history of his family.

◈ Bronze casting

The ancient Chinese cast pots with detailed patterns. To do this, they first made an exact model of the vessel in clay or **loess**. Once this had hardened, they packed more loess around the model to form the mould. They removed the mould in sections and also made a 'core', a loose piece that fitted inside the vessel to create the empty space. Once the sections and core had been **fired**, they were ready to use. Liquid bronze, made by heating copper and tin, was poured into the mould and left to cool. Each mould was reusable and could be used to make many models. Moulds could also be made out of wax. Although wax moulds were not reusable, they could produce finer detail. Wax moulds are still used today.

21

Working in iron

Although bronze was sometimes used to make temple statues of the Buddha or **bodhisattvas**, it was usually too expensive. Iron, on the other hand, was plentiful and cheap. It was often cast to make large models of animals and humans, like this cast-iron guardian figure. The figures were painted using a layer of **gesso** first so that the paint would stick.

Bronze mirrors

As the Chinese did not master glass making until the Qing dynasty (1644–1911), the first mirrors were made of bronze. Mirrors were used from Shang times. One side was highly polished, while the other side might be decorated or inscribed with a special message that protected the mirror's owner.

Silver and gold

At first, silver and gold were used to make small items, such as decorative belt buckles, or to **inlay** objects made of bronze. In Hebei province, in the tomb of a king from the 4th century BCE, archaeologists found the skeletons of two hunting dogs, each wearing an ornate collar made of silver and gold!

From the 7th century, gold and silver were often used to make artefacts for **Buddhist** temples, especially **reliquaries** (caskets in which holy relics are kept). During Tang and Song times, gold and silver were worked to make **intricate** crowns, hairpins, and combs, sometimes inset with precious gems. The very richest families even commissioned stunning sets of silver or gold tableware.

Silver and gold work are still produced today. Yellow gold is traditionally worn by and given to Chinese brides, while silverware is used for a host of decorative items, including vases, ornate plates, goblets, trays, incense burners, and other ornaments.

Made for an empress around 900 CE, this intricate gold crown is set with rubies and pearls.

◈ Decorative gold

Gold items made between the 7th and 13th centuries were often beautifully engraved, for example with animals or Buddhist symbols. To achieve the basic design, the gold was hammered out from the reverse side or pressed in a mould. Then the metalworker finished off the design on the right side, using a sharp engraving tool. This method is still used today to make ornate necklaces and crowns. Another traditional decorative technique is open-work, where skilful **artisans** pierce sheet gold over and over again, until it looks like lace.

Stone carving

Large stone sculptures of people and animals were an important feature of tomb complexes. Some of the oldest Chinese stone animals have been found on the tomb mound of a Han general called Huo Qubing, who died in 116 BCE. They include boars, elephants, horses, tigers, piglets, and fish. There is even a human figure wrestling with a bear. The style of carving means that some of the sculptures have kept their boulder form, but also look like animals – almost as if a beast is beginning to break free of the rock.

Built to impress

Many Song tombs (960–1279 CE) are attended by lifelike figures of foreign ambassadors, often carrying gifts. These sculptures aim to show how, because of their good relations with other countries, the Song had influence beyond China. The figures are really a display of power. As well as protecting the tombs, they are meant to impress the living.

The Spirit Way is a road that leads to the Ming tombs at Nanjing, in Jiangsu province. Built around the 15th century, it is flanked by enormous marble animals, both real and mythical. They include pairs of camels, elephants, lions, horses, the unicorn-like *xiezhi*, and a *qilin*, which has a horn on its head, a scaly body, a cow's tail, and the hooves of a deer. Further along the Spirit Way there are civil officials and giant stone soldiers in armour. Mining the rock and transporting it to the site must have been a huge job.

Power to the people!

From the 1950s, the Communist Party produced a new style of stone carving for public squares. Often made of concrete, a typical sculpture shows a group of larger-than-life workers or soldiers in heroic poses. As with the tomb sculptures, the idea is to put across a message of power and strength. Here, the power is shown to come from the people pulling together to make a contribution to the state.

Buddhist sculptures

The earliest **Buddhist** sculptures in China date from the 5th century CE. They are huge stone figures of the Buddha and **bodhisattvas** that were carved over several centuries.

Most of the sculptures in city temples were destroyed by anti-Buddhist emperors or in the early years of Communist rule. However, wonderful examples survive at remote cave temples – monasteries cut into cliff faces.

The caves at Yungang, near Datong in Shanxi province, contain over 50,000 sandstone statues. The first five caves have enormous Buddhas that were carved to look like five real Chinese emperors. At nearly 14 metres (46 feet) high, this colossal Buddha is the most massive of the carvings.

Precious jade

The Chinese are famous for their **jade**, a hard precious stone. The two different forms of jade, jadeite and nephrite, are made of different materials. Jadeite is usually found in varying shades of green, while nephrite is usually dark green but can also be creamy-white or grey. The Chinese used nephrite mined from Khotan, on the edge of the Taklimakan Desert, and Yarkand, which is in Xinjiang province. After 1750 CE, the Chinese also imported jadeite from Burma.

Around 4500 BCE, the Chinese began carving slabs of jade to make ceremonial weapons. They also fashioned simple jade animals, such as turtles, birds, elephants, and dragons.

Mysterious shapes

Some of the strangest and most plentiful Stone Age jade objects are a mystery. **Archaeologists** have found thousands of flat jade disks, called *bi*, and square tubes, called *cong*, mostly in tombs.

A craftworker carves jade in a Beijing workshop.

Working with jade

Jade is extremely tough; it takes great skill to carve it. The traditional way to work jade is by grinding rather than carving. **Artisans** use rough sand, which slowly smoothes the stone into shape. Today, some jade is worked by machine – the man on the left is carving an ornament using this technique – but the precious stone can damage even the hardest diamond-blade saws.

Jade suits

Jade's hardness and durability made it a symbol of immortality. Jade objects were placed in tombs to protect or preserve the dead. By Han times, the Chinese were burying important people in jade suits of armour. Nearly 50 of these suits have been discovered – they are made of thousands of small squares of jade, linked together with wire. The metal used for the wire was gold, silver, or copper, depending on the **rank** of the person. The jade burial suit shown below was made in the 2nd century BCE for a Han princess called Tou Wan.

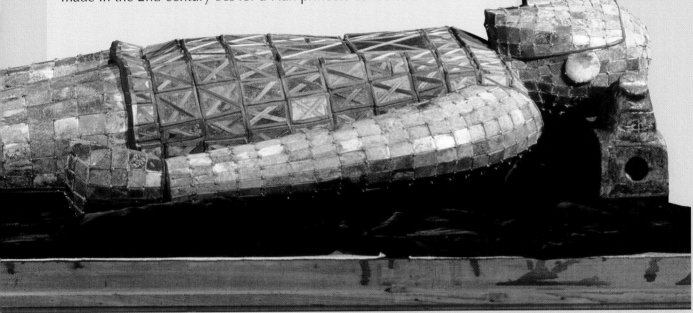

Both *bi* and *cong* have a round hole through the middle, but while some are smooth, others are carved with faces or monsters. They were probably **amulets** (protective charms) that formed part of a **ritual** connected with the dead, although no one knows why those two particular shapes were used.

Jade accessories

From Stone Age times until the present day, jade has been used to make treasured pendants, beads, and hair ornaments, such as combs. Jade bangles and rings, carved from a single piece of stone, are now very popular. They may be plain and simple or ornately carved.

Stone ornaments

Incense burners, inkstones (stones used in **calligraphy**), paperweights, and ornaments are made from all sorts of beautiful stones, including jade, soapstone, turquoise, and agate. Stones are also used to craft beautiful games pieces, for example for Chinese chess. Some craftspeople specialize in carving three-dimensional scenes that show mountains, trees, and rivers. These miniature worlds are sometimes known as fairy mountains and are meant to be objects of contemplation – owners gaze at them while meditating. However, not all miniature worlds are made of stone. Bone, ivory, **lacquer**, **bamboo** root, and **porcelain** are popular materials too.

Lacquerware and cork

Shiny, hardwearing lacquerware is a Chinese speciality made from the sap of the **lacquer** tree. The sap is naturally red, black, yellow, or green, but can be artificially coloured using dyes. The lacquer is applied, layer by layer, on to a base shape, often made of cloth-covered wood. Each thin layer has to harden and dry, which can take weeks, and is then polished before the next layer is applied. Some objects are built up from hundreds of layers of lacquer.

Painted lacquerware

The Chinese use lacquer to coat make-up boxes, trays, food containers, and musical instruments. In the period between 475 and 220 BCE, they even made lacquer coffins. Once the final, highly reflective surface has been built up, it is often painted with flowers, birds, dragons, and landscapes. Ancient lacquer coffins were painted with a picture of the dead person inside.

◈ Mother-of-pearl

Mother-of-pearl, or nacre, comes from certain mollusc shells and is the same material from which pearls are made. To harvest mother-of-pearl, first the outer surface of the shell is carefully cut away. Then the pale, inner shell is sliced into thin, flattish pieces, which are smoothed and polished.

To make it easier to cut the mother-of-pearl into particular shapes without it splitting, it is glued on to a thin piece of wood. The wood can be sawn into the right shapes, then peeled off the shell. Finally, the piece of shell is carefully set in place on the still-wet lacquer.

The milky gleam of the mother-of-pearl makes a good contrast to the dark wood of this screen. The decoration shows two dragons, symbols of imperial power.

Precious inlays

During the 7th and 8th centuries CE, lacquer artists often finished off their work with extravagant **inlays** of **mother-of-pearl**, gold, and silver, creating very detailed scenes. Mother-of-pearl was most popular in the early 17th century, when it was even used on luxurious lacquer screens. It is still popular today, but very few craftspeople are working with materials of high quality.

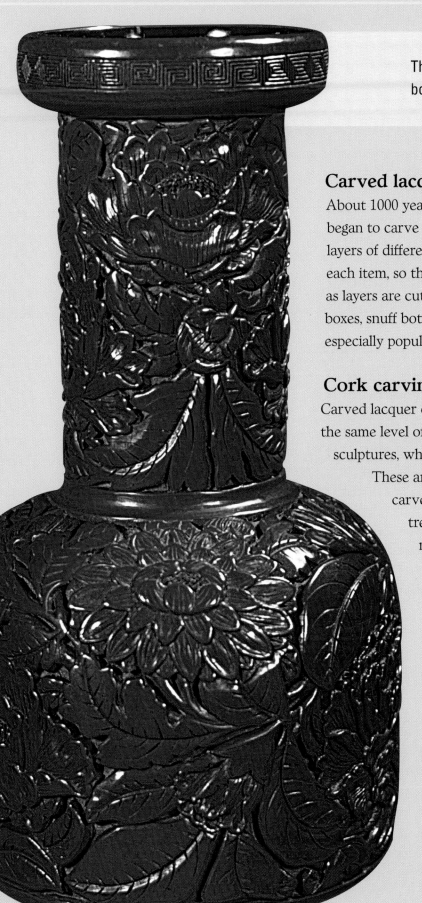

This 17th-century red lacquer bottle is carved with peonies.

Carved lacquerware

About 1000 years ago, Chinese craftspeople began to carve lacquer. Sometimes they use layers of different coloured lacquer to make each item, so that the colours are revealed as layers are cut away. Carved lacquerware boxes, snuff bottles, trays, and fan handles are especially popular today.

Cork carvings

Carved lacquer can be incredibly **intricate**, and the same level of detail is found in Chinese cork sculptures, which are also still made today. These are three-dimensional scenes carved out of the wood of the cork tree. Cork sculptures are left their natural colour, although most feature at least two white painted cranes. Cranes are very symbolic birds for the Chinese, representing long life, wisdom, and faithfulness.

Silk

China has been famous for its silk for thousands of years – the main trade route linking China to the West was even known as the Silk Road. The ancient Romans prized Chinese silk and imported both thread and cloth.

The Chinese kept their methods of silk production a closely guarded secret, so Westerners were unable to make their own. Knowledge of silk-making gradually spread west after two Persian monks smuggled some silkworm eggs out of China in the 6th century CE. However, China remained the world's key producer.

Beginnings of silk

The earliest surviving scraps of Chinese silk date back further than Roman times, to around 2700 BCE, but knowledge of silk-making probably came even earlier. **Archaeologists** have found a 6000-year-old ivory cup with a silkworm design, as well as parts of simple **looms** dating back 7000 years.

The Chinese have a story explaining how silk was first discovered. An emperor called Huang-ti wanted to know what was nibbling the leaves of his mulberry trees and his gardeners identified some silk moth caterpillars and their **cocoons**.

While Huangdi's wife, Xi Ling Shi, was looking at the cocoons, one fell into some hot water and started to unravel into fine silken fibre.

From cocoon to loom

The Chinese soon realized that it made sense to raise their own silkworms rather than try to collect them from the wild. So, silk was produced by government workshops and family businesses.

Once the fibre was harvested, several strands were twisted together to make threads thick enough for weaving. Using threads of different thicknesses, the Chinese could weave different silk cloths, from light gauzes to heavy **brocades**.

Traditionally, silk is woven by hand on a horizontal loom. The threads arranged lengthways on the loom are known as the warp threads and those arranged cross-ways are the weft threads. By choosing warp and weft threads of different colours, it is possible to weave different patterns or designs. Silk **damask**, for example, is a decorative fabric produced from contrasting warp and weft threads.

This 13th-century silk scroll shows a step in silk production.

◆ Silk production

The ancient Chinese method of silk-making, or sericulture, involved hatching lots of silk moth eggs all at the same time. The caterpillars were then kept on **bamboo** trays and fed hand-picked mulberry leaves. Some cocoons were allowed to develop into adult moths, so that they could produce more eggs. The rest were dropped into boiling water, which made each cocoon unwind to produce a single fibre that could be nearly a kilometre (over half a mile) long!

This factory worker is bundling up rolls of silk thread in Hangzhou, Zhejiang province. Known as the 'land of silk', Zhejiang today produces a third of China's raw silk.

The back of this 19th-century official court robe is embroidered with an imperial dragon.

Satin and velvet

Satin, with its smooth surface, was invented in China around the 12th century CE. Thick, luxurious velvet probably originated in Turkey or Italy, but was adopted in China by Ming times. The technique for velvet-making was probably passed on by Arabian silk traders.

Decorative silk

Silk tapestry, or *kesi*, appeared in China during the Tang **dynasty** around the 7th century CE. In silk tapestry, both the background fabric and the foreground threads are made of silk. Tapestry artists favoured big, bold designs without repeats. Like the painters of the day, they chose beautiful birds and flowers as their subjects. In time, *kesi* became the most prized of all Chinese textiles. Some of the most precious tapestries featured threads of real gold.

Plain silk fabric can be tie-dyed or printed. **Artisans** use simple printing blocks to create colourful, repeat designs. Far more luxuriously, silks can be hand-painted or **embroidered**. Some of the most beautiful examples of embroidered textiles are the pairs of **rank** badges that courtiers wore from 1391 until 1911. These were squares of embroidered or woven silk, which were sewn on to the front and back of their robes. They featured a particular animal, such as a dragon, leopard, or bird, that indicated the rank of the wearer. There were strict rules about what could be shown on a badge, even down to the number of claws on a dragon's feet.

Ancient dress

Embroidery reached its most ornate in the 'dragon robes' worn by Qing emperors and their officials. These informal garments were decorated with a large, hand-stitched dragon on the back.

With its flattering cut, the traditional *cheongsam* remains popular today in China and around the world. Many contemporary designers have found inspiration from its shape.

Summer robes were made from light, cool silk; those for winter wear were quilted – two layers of silk were stitched together with a thick layer of warm padding in between. Quilting is still a popular technique in modern China for creating cosy dresses and jackets.

Modern dress

In the 20th century, Chinese women adopted the *cheongsam* (known in Mandarin as the *qipao*). The *cheongsam* is a figure-hugging dress with a row of cloth-covered buttons at one shoulder. It can be knee-length or long and suits summer or winter wear, depending on the weight of the fabric. Most *cheongsams* are factory-made, with machined embroidery, but a few are made by hand.

◈ Applying colour

The Chinese traditionally use plant dyes to colour silk. Safflower, sappan wood, and madder produce reds and pinks; magnolia, indigo, and shikonin make blue and purple; gardenia and turmeric produce yellow; and tannin with iron makes brown and black. **Mineral** pigments, including gold, silver, lead, and mica, can be printed on to cloth to give areas of colour.

Paintings and calligraphy

Chinese painting began over 3000 years ago, during the Shang **dynasty**, when artists painted directly on to walls. The tradition of painting on silk emerged in the 3rd century BCE, with painters producing banners and scrolls. Works on paper did not become common until the 13th century. Even so, silk has remained a popular medium – especially for painted fans, which usually feature landscapes, birds, or flowers.

Wall paintings

Wall paintings by ancient Chinese artists have not survived very well. A few examples have been found in tombs but they just give a taste of how interiors may have looked. Palaces were probably adorned with colourful, handpainted **murals**. **Buddhist** cave temples from the 5th century CE also feature the faded remains of wall paintings.

Silk painters

Between the 4th and the 10th centuries, Chinese silk painters concentrated on the human figure – their clothes and movements are shown with graceful brush strokes. Many paintings tell stories that teach the viewer how to act. This sort of figure painting fitted in with the teachings of **Confucius**, which were popular at the time. He emphasized how important it was for people to behave well. Confucius also believed that harmony comes through relationships with other people.

Buddhist art

Some of the best examples of silk wall hangings have been found in Buddhist temples, especially the cave temples at Dunhuang, in Gansu province. They show the Buddha and **bodhisattvas**, as well as scenes of nirvana, or paradise. This late 9th-century painted-silk banner (left) from Dunhuang shows the bodhisattva Vajrapani, whose name means 'thunderbolt-bearer'. Painters also produced religious banners to cover coffins or for use in holy processions. These usually showed a single, dramatic figure of a god.

Landscape painting

Artists began to be interested in landscape painting during the Tang dynasty, in the 7th and 8th centuries, probably reflecting the influence of **Daoism**. The Daoists believed that it was important to be alone to think and muse on nature. Tang painters became famous for their landscapes in shades of blue and green. Sometimes, these landscapes featured human activities, such as journeys, but more often they just showed a single artist figure dreaming, or did not include any people at all. This painting is called *The Emperor Ming Huang Travelling in Shu*, and shows three scenes, to be read from right to left. It is a copy of a 7th-century blue-and-green landscape, made centuries later. The original is lost.

◈ Shifting perspective

In Western art, **perspective** was developed during the early 15th century. Artists imagined the viewer standing at a particular spot in front of the painting and then indicated distant objects by painting them smaller, and by making sure that they appeared along one of the viewer's 'sight lines' to the horizon. Chinese artists have a different tradition. They use a technique called 'shifting perspective' and do not assume the viewer will stay in a fixed point. Instead, the artist encourages the viewer to let their eyes flit about.

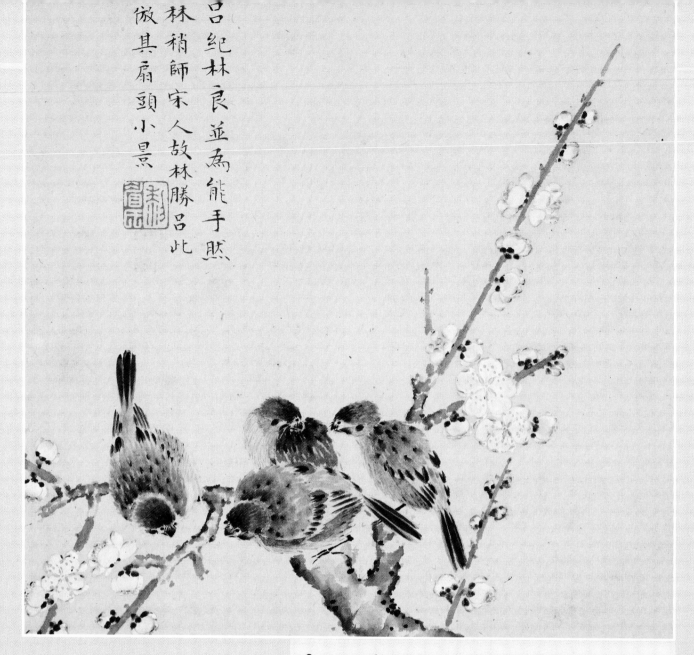

倣其扇頭小景
林稍師宋人故林勝呂此
呂紀林良並為能手然

Seventeenth-century artist Zhou Xianji painted these
plum blossoms and sparrows in ink on paper.

A painter's aims

In the 6th century CE, the writer Xie He recorded what he considered to be the six ingredients that made a good painting. Above all, he prized energy and vitality, where the artist really caught the spirit (or *qi*) of his subject. He thought this was more important than producing an exact copy of a particular landscape or object. For this reason, most Chinese painters prefer to paint from the imagination because it allows them to get closer to capturing the essence of a landscape.

It is amazing that an idea written down 1500 years ago is still meaningful to today's artists. Xie He's other points are just as relevant. They include the strength of the composition (how the elements of the picture are arranged) and the importance of copying earlier paintings. Whereas Westerners emphasize originality, Chinese painters have a long tradition of revisiting old styles and subject matter. This is a way of showing respect for previous master painters.

This mountain scene is from an album of eight landscapes by Shen Zhou (1427–1509).

Painting on paper

Around the 13th century, artists began to work on paper rather than silk. At first, paper was just a cheap alternative, but soon painters preferred it. As paper absorbs ink well without it running, artists suddenly had a lot more freedom.

Many of the first paintings on paper were made for albums. These were collections of six to twelve paintings, stuck together to create a concertina shape. A single album could feature more than one artist.

Like ancient **handscrolls**, albums allowed the viewer to get close to a painting. Looking at art in this way was a private experience. Popular subjects included studies of flowers, birds, butterflies, or **bamboo**. These remain traditional subjects for Chinese painters.

Brush strokes

A painter captures the life spirit or *qi* of a painting through his brush strokes. These can be narrow, quick, and urgent or broad and sweeping. In the 13th century, Chan monks, who belonged to a strict Buddhist sect, developed their own style of painting, using simple compositions and carefully controlled brush work. The best-known Chan artists are Liang Kai and Mu Qi. They created direct, uncomplicated works that were very different from the court paintings of the time, and they still inspire artists today.

◈ Paper making

Paper was invented around 105 CE, probably by a eunuch called Cài Lún. It was usually made from stems of bamboo, or wood from the paper mulberry tree, which were soaked, pounded, and boiled up with lime. After more pounding, the plant fibres were used to coat a bamboo screen. Pressed and dried, this became a sheet of paper.

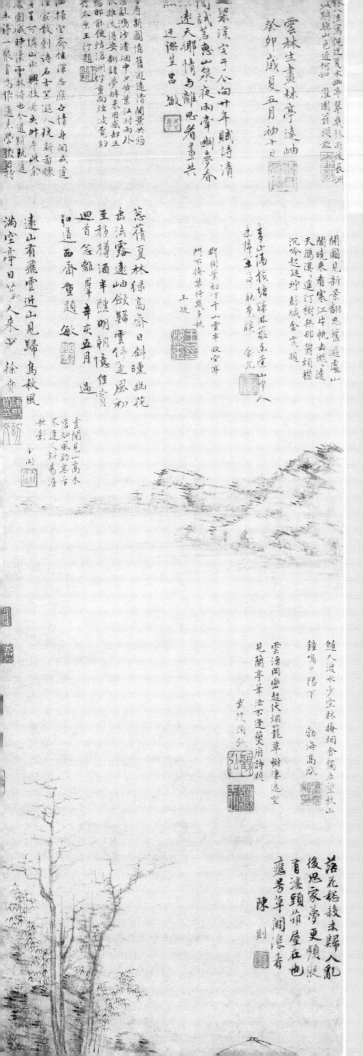

The calligraphy complements the landscape in this work by Ni Zan (1301–74). It is called *Grove of Trees, **Pavilion** and Distant Peaks*. Seal stones, or 'chops', have been used to sign this piece of art.

History in writing

Writing is so important to the Chinese that their word for culture is *wenhua*, which means 'to be able to read and write'. Chinese written records stretch back 3000 years – longer than for any other culture. Until 1949, Chinese written characters had hardly changed since the rule of the first Qin emperor, who tried to preserve them. As a result, scholars today can read the inscriptions on ancient monuments or read poems as they were written centuries ago.

The art of calligraphy

Calligraphy is beautiful, decorative handwriting. Temples and homes all over China are decorated with pieces of calligraphy. The calligrapher chooses a phrase or idea to represent, then he or she tries to make the brush strokes put across the idea of the characters (writing). This could be an idea from nature or mythology, such as 'leaping dragon', or it could be a religious saying.

Artists and calligraphers often sign their works with a special representation of their name, called a 'chop'. This is printed with their seal stone – a stone printing block. Seal stones can be works of art in themselves, often made of marble or **jade**.

Words and pictures

For the Chinese, the arts of painting and calligraphy are closely linked. In both, the brush strokes and tones of the ink are important. Not surprisingly, a painting style developed from the 8th century CE that brought these complementary arts even closer together. Painters began to add calligraphy inscriptions – columns of Chinese characters – to their paintings.

Painting and calligraphy today

During the 20th century, Chinese painters experimented with Western painting styles, but they did not abandon their centuries of tradition. Today's artists are still producing landscapes and figure paintings in careful brushwork. However, they also feel free to mix ancient and modern.

For example, artist Zhang Xiaogang (b.1958) does not paint in traditional inks on paper or silk. Instead, he paints in oils on canvas, influenced by painting styles of the West. However, he also incorporates his Chinese heritage by including inscriptions in Chinese characters.

Calligraphy is a highly respected Chinese tradition.

The 'four treasures'

A calligrapher has four tools of the trade, known as the 'four treasures': brush, ink, inkstone, and paper. The brush is usually made of goat-hair, attached to a bamboo tube. The ink is made from glue, carbon, and lampblack – a kind of oil – which is usually moulded into a cake and dried. Some ink cakes are shaped in decorative moulds that show detailed scenes. To use the ink, the calligrapher rubs the cake into the inkstone, which is a piece of stone with a small hollow in the middle. Then he or she mixes the powdered cake with a little water.

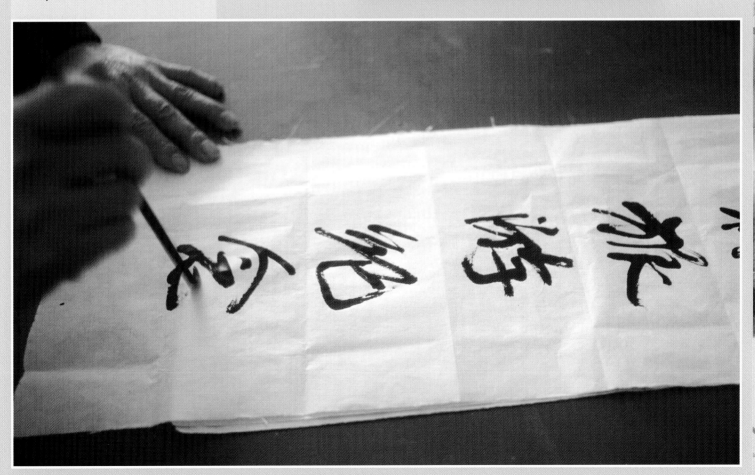

Woodblock prints

Printing was invented in China during the Tang dynasty, in the 8th century CE. At first, it was used to reproduce important **Buddhist** texts and images. This meant that holy works could spread much more quickly, because they no longer needed to be copied out by hand.

The Diamond Sutra

Although there are some earlier examples of block-printed books from China, *The Diamond Sutra* is the earliest that has a date on it (868 CE). It was found in the Caves of the Thousand Buddhas near Dunhuang. No one is sure where it was printed, but Sichuan, in southwestern China, was an important centre of printing at that time. The quality of the printing suggests that it was produced by a very experienced and skilful **blockcutter**.

The printing process

Printing was carried out in workshops. The blockcutter had to carve a mirror image of the text or pictures on to wooden blocks. Ink was brushed on to the printing block, then a sheet of paper was placed on top. Finally, it was brushed so that the text or image was transferred.

Colour printing did not become common until the 17th century. It was more expensive than black-and-white printing. The blockcutter had to carve a block for each colour, sometimes as many as ten, and the paper had to be carefully positioned on each block as the colour was transferred. If any of the blocks were not in exactly the right position, the finished picture would be blurred – and ruined.

The opening page of *The Diamond Sutra* features a finely detailed woodblock print showing the Buddha surrounded by his followers.

New Year pictures

The tradition of putting up prints to mark the lunar New Year has been going on for more than 700 years. Chinese New Year starts on the first day of the Chinese calendar, usually in February. On New Year's Eve, families decorate the walls of their homes with woodblock prints of household gods or lucky mascots as a way of welcoming in the god of wealth. The tradition is popular today, but it was most widely practised during Qing times, when the range of prints was enormous. Some prints showed workers going about their everyday tasks, while others illustrated popular fairy tales, or showed fruit or flowers.

Outside influences

During the 18th century, some Chinese printers adopted a new technique from Europe – copperplate engraving. An image etched on to a copper printing plate could be more finely detailed than one on a wooden printing block.

However, block printing was given new life in the 20th century. In the 1920s, a new art style was born, known as the Modern Woodcut Movement. The artists involved used ancient block-printing techniques to produce very startling new images, usually showing the gritty hardships suffered by workers.

◈ Rubbings

Long before printing was invented, the Chinese used rubbings to copy words and pictures that had been etched or moulded on to metal or **ceramics**. First, they moulded a sheet of damp paper over the surface to be rubbed. Then they dabbed the paper all over with an ink-soaked silk pad.

This colourful New Year woodcut print is taken from *Three Nuns of Xiangshan*.

41

Musical instruments

Music has been part of Chinese life and culture for thousands of years. Some of the most ancient instruments found by **archaeologists** include clay *ocarinas* (small, round, egg-shaped flutes), stone chimes, and sets of bronze bells. No ancient drums survive, but there are written references to them on **oracle bones**. They were probably made of wood and animal skins.

A young Naxi man plays the *pipa*. The Naxi people live in Yunnan and Sichuan provinces. They are descended from Tibetan nomads.

According to legend, harmony was invented in 2697 BCE, when the emperor Huang-ti sent the scholar Ling Lun into the mountains to cut **bamboo** pipes. Ling Lun's pipes mimicked the twelve notes produced by the phoenix bird, creating the very first music scale. Chinese music has totally different scales and harmonies from music of the Western world and has also developed its own very complex system of notation (how the music is written).

Plucked strings

The *qin* is a type of zither that has been played in China for at least 3000 years. It has seven silk or metal strings and a long **soundbox**, with marks showing the positions of thirteen particular pitches. The *qin* was a favourite instrument of scholar-poets because its plucked strings create **ethereal** notes. In keeping with **Daoist philosophy**, the silences are considered as important as the sounds.

Sometimes a *qin* player sings ancient poems or is accompanied by a kind of flute. In 1425, the Ming prince Zhu Quan wrote down music for the *qin* in his *Shenqi mipu* (Wondrous and Secret Notation). Some of today's *qin* musicians play instruments that date back over 1200 years, to Tang times.

The *zheng* is another type of Chinese zither used to play musical styles that originated in imperial China. Shorter than the *qin*, the *zheng* has sixteen or more strings and is usually accompanied by the flute, fiddle and *pipa*, which is a pear-shaped lute with four strings.

Folk music for ceremonies

In China, occasions such as weddings and funerals are usually attended by *chuigushou* bands – literally, 'blowers and drummers'. The blowers play the *suo na*, an oboe that flares out at the end. As well as drums, the band may include other **percussion** instruments, such as woodblocks.

Musical materials

The Chinese sometimes classify instruments according to what they are made of rather than how they produce sound. Leather, wood, stone, and metal are all used for making instruments. In southern China, there is even a style of music called *sizhu*, or 'silk and bamboo'. *Sizhu* bands feature bamboo flutes and Chinese fiddles or banjos with silk strings.

This Chinese mouth organ, or *sheng*, consists of seventeen bamboo pipes.

43

Dance and drama

Dance is an important part of Chinese culture, and is used to entertain as well as to mark special occasions, such as New Year. It is also one of the key ingredients of Chinese opera, which is really an all-round dramatic event, involving sections of speech, music, acrobatics, and pantomime – even displays of **martial arts**.

New Year celebrations

Chinese dancers mark celebrations throughout the year, but the most famous dances are performed at New Year. The Chinese follow a lunar calendar, based on the movements of the Moon rather than the Sun. This means that the exact date of the Chinese New Year changes each year, but it usually occurs some time in February. Two of the most popular New Year dances are the lion dance and the dragon dance.

The lion dance

Two dancers take part in the lion dance, one is at the head of the costume and one at the tail. The lion is traditionally made of silk, with silken tassels. Sometimes its facial features can be controlled from inside, so the dancer can make the lion open and close its eyes, for example.

During the dance, the dancers make the lion perform a series of movements, accompanied by **percussion** instruments such as drums, cymbals, and gongs. Near the end of the dance, the lion pretends to eat the lucky bundle of leaves and money that is hanging from a doorway, then dramatically spits out the leaves. This is a sign that there will be plenty of food and riches in the year ahead.

The dragon dance

The other dance that brings good luck for the coming year is the dragon dance. Some dragons are exceptionally long, requiring teams of 50 people or more to control them. The dancers make set movements, leaping and crouching to the beat of the drum. A skilful team of dancers can make the dragon form special patterns – these have names such as 'cloud cave' or 'going around the pillar'.

Other dances

There are many other traditional dances in China, some of which are regional. Waist-drum dancing is popular in parts of northern China. The dancers usually dress as soldiers in military-style costumes and wear drums strapped to their waists. They make the beat of their drums sound like the thundering of horses' hooves.

The fan dance used to be performed by dancing girls to entertain the emperor. Each dancer would hold a fan and make special arm movements, while the rest of her body hardly moved. Dances like this are still sometimes performed to mark national holidays. Other ancient forms of entertainment, such as acrobatics and circus, remain popular too.

◈ Dragons

In Chinese mythology, the dragon is an important symbol of supernatural power. During celebrations and parades, people often wave a paper dragon with a pearl in its mouth. The pearl represents wisdom and light.

At these New Year celebrations in China's capital, Beijing, a pair of lions performs the lion dance.

45

This opera player's black-and-white painted face symbolizes bravery and cunning.

 ## Making up

All the actors in a Chinese opera wear colourful and dramatic make-up. However, for the actor playing the 'painted-face' character – a god or a warrior – make-up is especially important. The colour of his face gives the audience a clue to his personality. A red face means loyalty, black means bravery, white can mean cunning, and yellow means likely to act without thinking.

A long history

The tradition of Chinese opera stretches back nearly 1000 years. Long ago, operas were performed by travelling troupes of actors and performances could go on for days. Today, the best-known opera in China is the Beijing Opera. However, other styles have developed in different parts of the country, each with its own traditions, costume styles, and stories.

Each opera tells a well-known story. The actors' elaborate costumes and colourful make-up tell the audience what kinds of characters they are playing – usual characters include gods, warriors, clowns, and lovers.

All the actors' movements are very stylized and have particular meanings. For example, if a character walks in a circle, it means he is going on a journey.

Apart from the amazing costumes, Chinese opera is performed with few props. Usually the stage is bare apart from a painted backdrop, although tables or chairs are sometimes used to represent a particular place such as a mountain, building, or throne.

A Chinese opera is accompanied by music from a range of instruments, including drums, **bamboo** flutes, the *sheng* (mouth organ) and the *pipa* (lute). In Beijing Opera, dramatic moments are usually marked by loud cymbal-clashes. The orchestra sits next to the stage, so the musicians can see the action and react quickly.

Shadow puppets

Another ancient form of theatre popular in China is the shadow play. The first shadow puppets were made of wood, but from the 12th century leather or paper became popular. Each puppet is **intricately** cut to create the shape of the character, then dyed, so that the shadow it casts is slightly coloured. The puppets' shadows are projected on to a screen, by having a light shone from behind them.

Shadow plays usually tell favourite stories about gods and heroes, and traditional tales from Chinese folklore. They first became popular during the Song **dynasty**, but according to legend shadow theatre began in China as long ago as 100 BCE. These shadow puppets from the late 1800s (below) show a well-dressed clown carried on a pole as if it were a sedan chair. The puppeteer would raise a laugh by showing the clown desperately trying to keep his balance!

Cross-currents

China's earliest contact with the rest of the world was via the Silk Road, along which Chinese silks were transported through the Middle East and into Europe. In return, traders brought foreign goods, such as wool, glass beads, silver, and gold into China.

By land and sea

In the 1270s CE, the Italian explorer Marco Polo reached China. Around this time, China was part of the Mongol Empire, which stretched across most of Central Asia. The Mongols helped to spread Chinese inventions, such as paper, westwards. Although Marco Polo had reached China over land, most of its contact with the rest of the world at that time was by sea.

The Chinese navy, which had been established in 1145, sailed to Japan and Korea, Southeast Asia, India, East Africa, and the Persian Gulf. China had a huge influence on Japan and Korea. As well as Chinese **ceramics** and **lacquerware**, these countries imported other aspects of Chinese culture, such as music, dance traditions, and religious beliefs.

Oriental exports

During the 16th century, the Portuguese and Spanish began to trade with China, providing huge amounts of silver in return for Chinese **porcelain** and lacquerware. By the 17th century, the finest kings and queens of Europe were eager collectors of Chinese porcelain. Soon, Chinese-style ceramics were being made in Europe – at Staffordshire in England, Delft in Holland, and Meissen in Germany.

During the 18th and early 19th centuries, there was a craze for all things Chinese. As well as drinking Chinese tea from porcelain tea services, rich Europeans built exotic **pavilions** and **pagodas** in their country parks and gardens. They filled their drawing rooms with **embroidered** silks, **bamboo** screens and handpainted wallpaper showing Chinese scenes. Known as **chinoiserie**, the Chinese style for interiors became popular again in the 1930s.

Trade between China and the West centered on the open port of Shanghai. Between the 1840s and 1940s, offices were established there by companies from many different countries, including Britain, France, Japan, Italy and the United States.

Chinese immigrants

The 19th and 20th centuries were times of great hardship in China. Many people chose to leave and make new lives in other countries, helping to spread Chinese culture further afield. Chinese food is now enjoyed around the world, while its dress styles have inspired international fashion designers. Most major cities have their own 'Chinatown', where traditional dragon dances can be seen each Chinese New Year.

Fashionable beliefs

Many people in the West now put their faith in Chinese medicine, or find out about their fortunes from their Chinese horoscope. Feng shui, a way of living based on ancient Chinese **philosophies**, has become increasingly popular. Followers of feng shui, which actually means 'wind and water', try to order their lives and possessions in order to achieve perfect harmony.

he Royal Pavilion in Brighton, England, built
y the Prince Regent (later George IV), has a
hinese-style music room. Decorated in 1815,
e walls were painted with Chinese scenes.
he room is lit by lotus-shaped chandeliers.

Foreign influences

During its long history China has borrowed and adapted many foreign ideas. As far back as the Bronze Age, Chinese metalworkers were copying the weapon styles and pot shapes used by neighbouring peoples. At the height of Silk Road trade, the Chinese began to keep fine horses, which they must have bought from Arab traders. These horses soon began to feature in their ceramic sculptures and paintings.

The 18th and 19th centuries were China's golden age of trade with Europe, when it was exporting enormous quantities of silk and porcelain to the West. In return, arts such as copperplate engraving were introduced to China. The Chinese government, however, was keen to keep influence from other countries to a minimum. Foreign traders were allowed no further than the port of Canton (present-day Guangzhou). The rest of China was closed to them.

However, it was impossible to ban the Chinese people from having access to other cultures, or their ideas. During the 19th century, Chinese intellectuals began to read Western books and soon they were questioning the power of the emperor and the structure of their society. This eventually led to the collapse of the Qing **dynasty**.

This 8th-century **glazed** figure shows a Silk Road trader riding on a camel. China's earliest contact with the West was with Arab traders.

In recent years, Chinese cinema has become more popular in the West. Zhang Yimou's 2002 film *Hero* was an international success.

The 20th and 21st centuries

As China struggled to rebuild itself, it borrowed all sorts of foreign ideas. Politicians introduced reforms based on what they had seen in other countries, such as education for women. Even the political system that China eventually adopted, Communism, was imported. Communism is based on the writings of the German philosopher Karl Marx and was first put into practice in Russia.

Under Communism, artists were encouraged to try out new, foreign art styles. Socialist Realism was a particular style of art that had already been popular in Russia. Rather than producing traditional paintings of perfect landscapes, artists showed industry, workers, and soldiers instead.

In recent decades, China has become even more open to outside influences. Chinese people enjoy wearing foreign fashions and watching foreign movies, while their artists work in new media – taking photographs or producing installations. The old styles are still popular and alive, but they are being blended with fresh influences from all over the world.

Chinese dynasties

Often, events in Chinese history are not referred to by the date on which they took place. Instead, we talk about which dynasty was in power at the time. Here is a list of the most important Chinese dynasties, along with the dates of their rule. After 1911, the Republicans ousted the emperor. In 1949, the Communists took power. They are still in control of the country.

Shang (*c.*1500–1050 BCE)

Zhou (1050–221 BCE)

Qin (221–207 BCE)

Han (206 BCE–220 CE)

Tang (618–906)

Song (960–1279)

Yuan (1279–1368)

Ming (1368–1644)

Qing (1644–1911)

Further resources

More books to read

Allan, Tony, *20th Century Perspectives: The Rise of Modern China* (Heinemann Library, 2003)

Anderson, Dale, *History in Art: Ancient China* (Raintree, 2004)

Higginbottom, Trevor, *Country Studies: China* (Heinemann Library, 2000)

Martell, Hazel Mary, *Looking Back: Imperial China from 221 BCE to CE 1294* (Evans Brothers, 1998)

Nicholson, Robert and Claire Watts, *Ancient China* (Franklin Watts, 1991)

Odijk, Pamela, *The Ancient World: The Chinese* (Heinemann Library, 1991)

Waterlow, Julia, *Look into the Past: The Ancient Chinese* (Wayland, 1994)

Websites

http://chineseculture.about.com
The latest news about Chinese culture

http://afe.easia.columbia.edu/song/
How life during the Song dynasty can be seen through a piece of artwork

http://www.museumca.org/exhibit/exhib_forbiddencity.html
An insight into the Forbidden City

http://www.asia.si.edu/collections/chineseHome.htm
A general site about Chinese art

http://www.walkthewall.com
Stunning pictures of the Great Wall of China

Places to visit

UK

The Ashmolean Museum, Oxford

The Bowes Museum, Barnard Castle, County Durham

The Burrell Collection, Pollok Country Park, Glasgow

The Ivy Wu Gallery of East Asian Art, Royal Museum, Edinburgh

Joseph E. Hotung Gallery of Oriental Antiquities, British Museum, London

The Museum of East Asian Art, Bath

The Oriental Museum, Durham

Percival David Foundation of Chinese Art, London

The Tsui Gallery, V&A Museum, London

USA

Fogg Art Museum, Harvard University

Freer and Sackler Galleries, Smithsonian Institute, Washington D.C.

Museum of Fine Arts, Boston

William Rockhill Nelson Gallery and Atkins Museum of Fine Arts, Kansas City

Australia

Chinese Museum, Melbourne

The Golden Dragon Museum, Bendigo, Victoria

Glossary

abstract describes art that does not imitate the world around us, that shows ideas rather than objects

amulet lucky charm

archaeologist someone who studies human beings and the way they live, especially past cultures

artisan craftworker

bamboo tall grass that grows in eastern Asia

blockcutter someone who carves wooden printing blocks

bodhisattva Buddhist saint

brocade heavy silk fabric with a raised design

Buddhism religion based on the teachings of the Buddha. Its followers strive to reach a state of total understanding and peace.

calligraphy the art of beautiful writing. Rather than using an alphabet of letters that stand for sounds, the Chinese write using picture-like symbols, called characters, which can stand for whole words or ideas.

cast make metal into a particular shape

ceramic material that is shaped and then hardened by firing – usually pottery, but also other materials such as enamel

chinoiserie describes an art or craft object that borrows Chinese decorative styles or motifs

cloisonné decorative enamel, where the sections of coloured enamel are divided by small strips of metal

cocoon silken covering made by a caterpillar when it is about to change into its adult form – a winged moth or butterfly

Confucianism belief system in which rituals and good behaviour help to create an ordered society

damask fabric, usually silk, with a woven pattern

Daoism belief system in which people try to understand the central life force, or *qi*, that flows through all of creation

dialect variety of a language that is spoken in a particular region

dynasty royal family of rulers

eave edge of a roof that sticks out further than the building below

embroidery decorative needlework or stitching

enamel metallic compound that can be fired to produce glossy, coloured decoration

ethereal delicate, light, and magical

ethnic relating to a particular race or cultural group of people

firing the process of hardening a ceramic material, such as pottery, by heating it in an oven called a kiln

gesso watered-down plaster or glue that is sometimes applied to a surface so that paint will stick to it better

glaze glassy coating often applied to pottery when it is being fired

handscroll rolled-up painting on silk or paper that fitted into the viewer's hand. Most handscrolls were long, so the viewer could see only a part of the painting at a time.

immortal god that exists for ever

inlay small piece of material, for example ivory or jade, that is inserted into an object as decoration

intricate complex

jade hard precious stone that is usually green

kaolin fine, soft white clay, used for making porcelain and china

kiln big furnace in which pottery can be fired

lacquer sap of the lacquer tree, which can be built up in layers to produce a very shiny, hard material

loess loose, wind-blown clay soil

loom machine for weaving

martial arts ancient ways of training the body and mind for better control of oneself. They can be used for actual fighting or in a stylized form for athletic competitions where the opponent is not actually hurt.

meditation deep thought

mineral substance that is not organic (not produced by a living animal or plant) and that is usually mined from the ground, for example types of rock

mother-of-pearl another name for nacre, the pearl coating that lines the shells of some molluscs (shellfish)

mural wall painting

oracle bone animal bone that was inscribed with writings in ancient China. Oracle bones were used in rituals to predict the future.

pagoda Buddhist tower, made up of lots of storeys with overhanging roofs

patriotic loyal to one's country

pavilion building with a roof but no walls. Posts support the roof.

percussion describes musical instruments that are played by hitting them, including drums

perspective the way an artist draws objects in space, in order to suggest their size and how near or far away they are

philosopher thinker who examines human beliefs and ways of thinking

plateau high area of level land

porcelain fine, white ceramic, originally from southern China

rank position in society

reliquary casket or box in which holy relics or souvenirs are kept

ritual special ceremony

soundbox body of a musical instrument that makes the sound louder, or amplifies it

stoneware a coarse kind of glazed pottery

taotie pattern of decoration that was abstract, but suggested the face of a monster

terracotta (1) unglazed, fired pottery (2) particular orangey-red clay

versatile useful in many different ways

vessel container or pot

Index